T0108467

POPSICLE PARTY

POPSICLE PARTY

HOME-MADE NATURAL ICED TREATS

Louise Pickford
photography by Ian Wallace

RYLAND PETERS & SMALL
LONDON • NEW YORK

Senior Designer
Sonya Nathoo
Commissioning Editor
Alice Sambrook
Production Manager
Mai-Ling Collyer
Editorial Director
Julia Charles
Art Director
Leslie Harrington
Publisher
Cindy Richards

Photographer
Ian Wallace
Food & Prop Stylist
Louise Pickford
Indexer
Vanessa Bird

First published in 2019 by
Ryland Peters & Small
20-21 Jockey's Fields
London WC1R 4BW
and
341 E 116th Street
New York, 10029
www.rylandpeters.com

10 9 8 7 6 5 4 3 2 1

Text copyright © Louise Pickford 2019
apart from Page 21: Probiotic Pumpkin
Popsicles by Dunja Gulin; Page 22:
Dairy-free Orange Creamsicles by Jenna
Zoe; Page 34: Peach and Plum Popsicles by
Sunil Vijayakar; Page 45: Avocado
Milkshake Popsicles by Tori Haschka;
Page 61: Coconut Frozen Yogurt with
Strawberries, Page 62: Sugar-free Mojito
Sorbet and Page 58: Cashew Butter Ice
Cream by Jordan Bourke

Design and photographs copyright
© Ryland Peters & Small 2019
All photography by Ian Wallace apart
from Page 20 by Toby Scott

The authors' moral rights have
been asserted. All rights reserved.
No part of this publication may be
reproduced, stored in a retrieval system
or transmitted in any form or by any
means, electronic, mechanical,
photocopying or otherwise, without the
prior permission of the publisher.

ISBN: 978-1-78879-089-5

A CIP record for this book is
available from the British Library. US
Library of Congress CIP data has been
applied for.

Printed in China

CONTENTS

INTRODUCTION

There is little better than the refreshing taste of a frozen popsicle when the weather is warm. Far from outdated, synthetic-tasting mass-produced versions, the new trend of gourmet popsicles range from healthy – packed with fresh fruits and vegetables, to indulgent – made with real chocolate and cream. They can be layered, coated, dipped or swirled to create beautiful effects and are equally perfect offered as instant treats or served as quirky dinner party desserts.

Making popsicles is easy, but first there are a few simple things to consider. Before you start, always consider the end – the freezer. Find a flat space in a drawer where your mould(s) can sit, or create a shelf with a large flat tray. Take your pick from the dedicated range of ice pop moulds available, which range in price and material, from silicone to plastic and even metal. If you don't have popsicle moulds, try using silicone baking moulds, cardboard espresso coffee cups, bamboo cones or plastic Champagne glasses instead. The moulds I have used in these recipes range from 100–150 ml/3^1/$_3$–5 fl oz. capacity, so you may need to alter recipe quantities slightly to fit the exact mould you have used. The classic wooden sticks can be bought separately, but some moulds come with their own re-usable plastic sticks. Sticks should be added to the mixture as soon as it is firm enough that they can stand up straight (the thicker the mixture, the sooner this will be), but you may need to freeze the ice pops for a little while first. The total freezing times depend on the ingredients you have used, the type of freezer you have and the size of your moulds. Hence, the freezing times given in this book are a guide and should be adjusted as needed.

When it is time to un-mould the little lovelies, silicone moulds can be pressed out, while other moulds will need to be dipped very briefly in hot water. Your popsicles can then be consumed, returned to the freezer to set a coating or stored for up to 3 months in plastic ziplock bags – ready for you to enjoy a popsicle party at a moment's notice!

HEALTHY

BEETROOT, ORANGE AND BLUEBERRY YOGURT SWIRLS

These delicious popsicles contain plenty of goodness from fresh fruits and exceptionally nutrient-rich beetroot/beet. They are sweetened with coconut flower syrup, which is a natural, low-GI syrup that has been used in Thai cooking for generations. It is sticky, so you may need to warm it through before using. It's available from health food or Asian food stores, but date syrup or honey are great alternatives.

500 g/generous 2 cups Greek yogurt

50 g/1¾ oz. coconut flower syrup (or date syrup or clear honey)

50 g/1¾ oz. raw beetroot/beet, finely grated

50 g/1¾ oz. fresh blueberries

freshly squeezed juice of 1 orange

1 tablespoon icing/confectioners' sugar

6 popsicle moulds and sticks

MAKES 6

Place the yogurt into a bowl and stir in the coconut flower syrup (or other sweetener). Pour the mixture into the six popsicle moulds.

Place the grated beetroot/beet, blueberries and orange juice in a blender and blend until really smooth. Add the icing/confectioners' sugar and blend again. Very carefully drizzle the beetroot/beet syrup into the moulds, swirling each one with a skewer to form ripples through the yogurt.

Add the sticks in an upright position at this stage, or freeze first for a while until the mixture is firm enough to hold the sticks straight. Freeze for 4–6 hours until frozen.

When you are ready to serve, dip the moulds into hot water for a second or two, then gently pull out the popsicles.

POWER-RICH POPSICLES

For all the gym junkies and fitness fanatics out there, these popsicles will give you an energy boost before, or nourishment after, a workout.

1 banana, peeled

250 g/9 oz. silken tofu, drained

250 ml/1 cup plus 1 tablespoon soya milk

60 ml/¼ cup coconut flower syrup (or date syrup)

2 tablespoons chia seeds

25 g/1 oz. goji berries, chopped, plus extra to serve

100 g/3½ oz. dark/bittersweet chocolate, melted

6 popsicle moulds and sticks

small baking sheet, lined with baking parchment

MAKES 6

Chop the banana and place in a blender with the tofu, soya milk and coconut flower syrup (or date syrup). Blend until smooth. Transfer the mixture to a bowl, then stir in the chia seeds. Refrigerate for 2 hours or until the seeds have swelled and softened.

Fold in the goji berries, then divide the mixture between the six popsicle moulds.

Add the sticks in an upright position at this stage, or freeze first for a while until the mixture is firm enough to hold the sticks straight. Freeze for 4–6 hours until frozen.

20 minutes before you are ready to serve, put the prepared baking sheet into the freezer.

After 10 minutes, dip the moulds into hot water for a second or two, then gently pull out the popsicles. Dip the ends of the popsicles into the melted chocolate. Place on the prepared chilled baking sheet and immediately scatter over the extra goji berries. Return to the freezer for a further 10 minutes to set.

MINT CHOCOLATE AND MATCHA STICKS

Matcha is the finely ground powder of green tea leaves, which are bursting with antioxidants. Here, matcha's earthy flavour marries well with mint and coconut milk for a delicious and healthy chilled treat.

400 ml/14 fl oz. can coconut milk

4 large fresh mint sprigs, bruised

1–2 teaspoon(s) good-quality matcha powder, plus extra to serve

4 tablespoons maple syrup or clear honey

50 g/1¾ oz. dark/bittersweet chocolate, chopped

melted dark/bittersweet chocolate, to serve

6–8 small or 4–6 large popsicle moulds and sticks

baking sheet, lined with baking parchment

MAKES 6-8 SMALL OR 4-6 LARGE

Combine the coconut milk and mint sprigs in a small saucepan over a medium heat. Bring the milk just to the boil, then remove from the heat and set aside until cold.

Strain the cold coconut milk, then whisk in the matcha powder and maple syrup (or honey) until completely dissolved. Refrigerate for about 1 hour until set enough to hold the chocolate pieces in place.

Fold the chocolate through the milk and then carefully spoon the mixture into the moulds. Add the sticks in an upright position at this stage, or freeze first for a while until the mixture is firm enough to hold the sticks straight. Freeze for 4–6 hours until frozen.

20 minutes before you are ready to serve, put the prepared baking sheet into the freezer.

After 10 minutes, quickly dip the moulds into hot water, then gently pull out the popsicles. Place the popsicles onto the prepared baking sheet and drizzle with melted chocolate. Dust with extra matcha powder and return to the freezer for 10 minutes to set before serving.

CRANBERRY, HONEY, GINGER AND LEMON SOOTHERS

You often hear that sipping a hot lemon, honey and ginger drink is the best way to soothe a sore throat and ward off a cold, but iced drinks are actually just as soothing. This popsicle version, enhanced with cranberry juice, is perfect for when you start feeling that tell-tale tickle at the back of your throat.

500 ml/2 cups plus 2 tablespoons water

250 ml/1 cup plus 1 tablespoon cranberry juice

30 g/1 oz. piece of fresh ginger, peeled and sliced

150 ml/⅔ cup clear honey

100 ml/⅓ cup plus 1 tablespoon freshly squeezed lemon juice (about 5 fresh lemons)

10 ice pop sleeves

funnel

MAKES 10

Place the water, cranberry juice and sliced fresh ginger in a small saucepan and bring slowly to the boil over a low-medium heat. Turn the heat down and let it simmer for 2 minutes, then add the honey and stir until dissolved.

Remove the pan from the heat and leave the mixture to cool to room temperature.

Strain the mixture to remove the ginger solids, then stir in the lemon juice.

Pour the liquid into the ice pop sleeves using the funnel and seal them closed. Freeze for 4–6 hours until frozen.

Snip the tops off the sleeves to enjoy the ice pops.

Tip: You can make these in regular ice pop moulds with sticks instead of in the sleeves, if you prefer.

ORANGE, MANGO AND CARROT STICKS

This is one of my favourite smoothie combinations in refreshing popsicle form. Carrots produce fairly sweet juice for a vegetable, so when combined with naturally sweet mangoes and orange juice, no extra sugar is required.

3 carrots, (about 300 g/10½ oz.)
1 ripe mango (about 450 g/1 lb.)
250 ml/1 cup plus 1 tablespoon freshly squeezed orange juice

juicer

6 popsicle moulds and sticks

MAKES 6

Top and tail and peel the carrots. Peel the mango and cut all the flesh away from the pit. Dice the flesh.

Using a juicer, extract all the juice from the carrots and place in a blender. Add the diced mango flesh and the orange juice and blend together until really smooth. Divide the juice between the six popsicle moulds.

Add the sticks in an upright position at this stage, or freeze first for a while until the mixture is firm enough to hold the sticks straight. Freeze for 4–6 hours until frozen.

When you are ready to serve, dip the moulds into hot water for a second or two, then gently pull out the popsicles.

BREAKFAST GRANOLA POPS

Your classic morning breakfast bowl of yogurt, granola, honey and fresh fruit in ice pop form! To be enjoyed at any time.

60 g/2¼ oz. granola

5 tablespoons clear honey

250 g/generous 1 cup Greek yogurt

150–200 g/5½–7 oz. prepared small fresh fruits such as grapes, strawberries, and/or kiwi, peeled and diced

50 g/1¾ oz. frozen or fresh raspberries, thawed if frozen

1 tablespoon icing/confectioners' sugar

6–8 popsicle moulds and sticks

small baking sheet, lined with baking parchment

MAKES 6-8

Place the granola in a bowl and stir in 2 tablespoons of the honey, and mix so that all the granola is really sticky. Divide the mixture between the moulds and press down firmly to compact the granola at the bottom. Freeze for 1 hour until really firm.

Place the yogurt in a bowl and stir in the remaining 3 tablespoons of honey. Spoon a little yogurt mixture into each mould and add some of the fresh fruits, alternating between the two until the moulds are full. Add the sticks in an upright position at this stage, or freeze first for a while until the mixture is firm enough to hold the sticks straight. Freeze for 4–6 hours until frozen.

Meanwhile, purée the raspberries in a blender with the icing/confectioners' sugar, then sieve/strain to remove all the seeds. Refrigerate.

20 minutes before you are ready to serve, put the prepared baking sheet into the freezer to chill. After 10 minutes, dip the moulds into hot water for a second or two, then gently pull out the popsicles. Place the popsicles on the prepared chilled baking sheet and immediately drizzle over the raspberry sauce. Return to the freezer for 10 minutes to set before serving.

PROBIOTIC PUMPKIN POPSICLES

Kombucha is a fermented tea drink that is rich in probiotics. Thanks to its amazing health benefits, it can now be found in most large grocery stores or supermarkets. It is lightly effervescent, which gives these popsicles a slightly fizzy taste.

240 g/2 cups raw pumpkin or butternut squash flesh, diced
480 ml/2 cups ready-made kombucha (lemon flavour or ginger flavour both work well)
2 tablespoons agave syrup
2 tablespoons freshly squeezed lemon juice

6–8 popsicle moulds and sticks

MAKES 6-8

Bring a pan of water to the boil. Add the diced pumpkin or squash, bring back to a simmer and cook for about 5 minutes or until just tender. Drain well, tip onto a plate and leave to cool completely.

Place the cooled pumpkin or squash cubes in a food processor with the kombucha, agave syrup and lemon juice and blend together until smooth and combined. Taste and adjust the amount of syrup and lemon to taste (the sweetness highly depends on the type of pumpkin or squash you have used).

Pour the mixture into the popsicle moulds. Add the sticks in an upright position at this stage, or freeze first for a while until the mixture is firm enough to hold the sticks straight. Freeze for 4–6 hours until frozen.

When you are ready to serve, dip the moulds into hot water for a second or two, then gently pull out the popsicles.

Tip: If you have a high-speed blender, you can simply blend the raw pumpkin or squash with the other ingredients, it tastes just as good!

DAIRY-FREE ORANGE CREAMSICLES

These popsicles are very easy to make and they taste luxuriously creamy. When blended and frozen, avocado and banana both have a smooth, rich texture without any help from traditional dairy cream, leading them to earn the nickname 'nice cream'.

1 ripe banana, peeled
and chopped
freshly squeezed juice
of 3 oranges (about
250 ml/1 cup plus
1 tablespoon), sieved/
strained
¼ ripe avocado, pitted
and peeled
250 ml/1 cup plus
1 tablespoon coconut
milk or almond milk
few drops of natural
vanilla extract

*10 popsicle moulds
and sticks*

MAKES 10

Simply combine all the ingredients in a blender and blitz until smooth. Transfer to a jug/pitcher and divide the mixture evenly between the popsicle moulds.

Add the sticks in an upright position at this stage, or freeze first for a while until the mixture is firm enough to hold the sticks straight. Freeze for 4–6 hours until frozen.

When you are ready to serve, dip the moulds into hot water for a second or two, then gently pull out the popsicles.

FRUITY

TUTTI FRUTTI POPS

Remember 'rockets', those multi-coloured popsicles from your childhood? This homemade version looks great and tastes even better.

250 g/1¼ cups caster/granulated sugar
500 ml/2 cups plus 2 tablespoons water
freshly squeezed juice of 2 oranges
freshly squeezed juice of 1 lemon
freshly squeezed juice of 2 limes
125 g/4½ oz. fresh raspberries

8 popsicle moulds and sticks

MAKES 8

Place the sugar and water in a pan and heat gently, stirring, until the sugar has dissolved. Turn up the heat and boil for 1 minute. Remove from the heat and leave to cool completely.

Place the orange, lemon and lime juices each in separate bowls and stir enough sugar syrup into each to give approx. 150 ml/⅔ cup liquid per bowl, with leftover syrup. (The exact amount of syrup you add will depend on how much juice your citrus fruits provide). Place the raspberries in a blender with 100 ml/⅓ cup plus 1 tablespoon of the remaining sugar syrup. Blend until very smooth. Taste for sweetness and add more syrup if needed.

Pour the orange syrup into each mould to fill about one quarter of the way up. Freeze for about 1 hour until completely set. Pour in the lime layer to fill about halfway up – either add the sticks at this stage or freeze until the mixture is firm enough to hold the sticks. Freeze again until firm and repeat the process, adding then freezing a raspberry layer, then finally adding the lemon layer to fill to the top. Freeze the ice pops for 4–6 hours until frozen.

When ready to serve, quickly dip the moulds into hot water, then pull out the popsicles.

REFRESHING APPLE AND CUCUMBER ICE POPS

The name of these says it all. They look really fun and are also great for kids who claim not to like cucumber... offer them one of these frozen treats and watch them change their mind!

4 apples
3 Lebanese cucumbers
freshly squeezed juice
    of 2 limes
100 g/½ cup caster/
    superfine sugar

juicer

*6–8 popsicle moulds
    and sticks*

MAKES 6-8

Cut one of the apples in half. Quarter, core and cut one of the halves into wafer thin slices, reserving the other half. Cut one of the cucumbers in half widthways and then cut one of the halves into wafer thin slices, reserving the other half. Set all the wafer thin slices of apple and cucumber aside for a moment.

Pass all the remaining apples and cucumbers and reserved halves through a juicer. Place the juice in a jug/pitcher and stir in the lime juice and sugar until the sugar has dissolved.

Divide the apple and cucumber slices between the moulds and fill to the top with the cucumber syrup. Add the sticks in an upright position at this stage, or freeze first for a while until the mixture is firm enough to hold the sticks straight. Freeze for 4–6 hours until frozen.

When you are ready to serve, dip the moulds into hot water for a second or two, then gently pull out the popsicles.

JUICY WATERMELON, STRAWBERRY AND LEMON POPS

All you need is a splash of vodka here and you'd have the perfect frozen daiquiri! But hey, who needs alcohol when you can enjoy this healthier fruit version in the form of an ice pop.

300 g/10½ oz.
   strawberries, hulled
   and halved
3 tablespoons icing/
   confectioners' sugar,
   sieved/strained
500 g/1 lb. 2 oz.
   watermelon
freshly squeezed juice
   of 1 lemon

*8–10 small popsicle
   moulds and sticks*

MAKES 8-10 SMALL

In a bowl, stir together the strawberries and sugar and leave for 1 hour for the strawberries to release their juices, stirring occasionally.

Cut away the watermelon rind and deseed and roughly dice the flesh.

Place the strawberries and all the juices, with the watermelon and lemon juice in a blender and blend until smooth. Divide the mixture between the popsicle moulds.

Add the sticks in an upright position at this stage, or freeze first for a while until the mixture is firm enough to hold the sticks straight. Freeze for 4–6 hours until frozen.

When you are ready to serve, dip the moulds into hot water for a second or two, then gently pull out the popsicles.

PURPLE PASSION POPS

These popsicles really have the wow-factor in terms of both vibrant taste and their almost fluorescent purple colour. The lime syrup will vary in sweetness/sharpness depending on the juice of the particular fruit you've used, so taste and add more sugar accordingly if needed.

250 ml/1 cup plus 1 tablespoon water

finely grated zest and freshly squeezed juice of 4 limes

200 g/1 cup caster/granulated sugar, plus extra to taste

250 g/9 oz. frozen mixed berries, thawed

8 popsicle moulds and sticks

MAKES 8

Combine the water, lime zest, lime juice and the sugar in a small saucepan over a low heat, stirring, until the sugar has dissolved. Taste and stir in a little more sugar if the syrup is too sharp, making sure it fully dissolves. Turn up the heat and bring to the boil for 1 minute, then remove the pan from the heat and allow the syrup to cool completely.

Place the mixed berries and the lime syrup into a blender and blend until completely smooth. Pour the mixture into the moulds. Add the sticks in an upright position at this stage, or freeze first for a while until the mixture is firm enough to hold the sticks straight. Freeze for 4–6 hours until frozen.

When you are ready to serve, dip the moulds into hot water for a second or two, then gently pull out the popsicles.

COCONUT, MANGO AND PASSION FRUIT POPSICLES

Indulge in the tropical taste of these layered fruit and coconut popsicles. I used bamboo cones lined with baking parchment as my moulds, but plastic Champagne glasses are also an excellent idea.

100 g/½ cup caster/
   granulated sugar
250 ml/1 cup plus
   1 tablespoon water
1 ripe mango (about
   450 g/1 lb.), peeled,
   pitted and flesh diced
1 tablespoon freshly
   squeezed lime juice
200 ml/generous ¾ cup
   coconut cream
200 ml/generous ¾ cup
   passion fruit pulp
   (from about 6 passion
   fruit)

*6–8 popsicle moulds
   and sticks*

MAKES 6-8

Place the sugar and water in a pan and heat gently, stirring, until the sugar has dissolved. Turn up the heat and boil for 1 minute. Remove from the heat and leave to cool completely.

Place the mango flesh in a blender with the lime juice and blend until smooth. Taste and add a little of the sugar syrup, if necessary. Whisk together the coconut cream with 1–2 tablespoons of the sugar syrup to your taste. Blend the passion fruit pulp with some of the remaining syrup to your taste.

Divide the passion fruit syrup between the moulds, filling a third of the way up and freeze for about 1 hour until firm. Next, add the coconut cream layer and freeze for about 30 minutes or until the mixture is firm enough to hold the sticks. Press the sticks in gently. Add the mango layer and freeze for a final 2–3 hours until frozen.

When you are ready to serve, dip the moulds into hot water for a second or two, then gently pull out the popsicles.

PEACH AND PLUM POPSICLES

A wonderfully refreshing and jewel-bright way to capture the warmth of summer with ripe, juicy peaches and plums.

600 g/21 oz. fresh
    peaches
600 g/21 oz. fresh plums
about 400 ml/scant 1¾
    cups water
caster/granulated sugar,
    to taste

12 popsicle moulds and
    sticks

small tray full of
    ice cubes

MAKES 12

Peel, pit and chop the flesh of the peaches and plums. Place the fruit into two separate saucepans, each with 200 ml/generous ¾ cup water and sugar to taste. Bring to the boil, reduce the heat to low and simmer gently for 4–5 minutes.

Place the peaches with their cooking water in a blender and process to a smooth purée, then set aside. Rinse out the blender and process the plums with their cooking water to a smooth purée. Let both purées cool.

Carefully spoon half of the peach purée into the base of the moulds and position them at an angle in the tray of ice. Freeze for 1 hour or until firm. Next, add the plum layer and freeze at an opposite angle for about 30 minutes or until the mixture is firm enough to hold the sticks. Press the sticks in gently. Add a final peach layer and freeze upright for a final 2–3 hours until solid. Note: You can switch up the order of the layers with plum-peach-plum instead, or as well, if you prefer.

When you are ready to serve, dip the moulds into hot water for a second or two, then gently pull out the popsicles.

POMEGRANATE, LIME AND ROSEWATER POPS

Pretty in pink may well have been the name of an 80s pop song, but it works equally well to describe these delicious and refreshing fruit popsicles. The rosewater is lovely with the flavour of the pomegranate and gives it that Middle Eastern allure.

4–5 pomegranates
freshly squeezed juice
   of 2 limes
30 g/2½ tablespoons
   caster/granulated
   sugar
2 teaspoons rosewater
fresh rose petals, dried
   rose petals and lime
   wedges, to decorate
   (optional)

*8 small popsicle moulds
   and sticks*

MAKES 8 SMALL

Cut the pomegranates in half over a bowl lined with a large sieve/strainer to catch the juices. Set half a pomegranate to one side. For the rest, squeeze out as much of the juice as you can from the seeds, pressing down on them with a metal spoon.

Measure out 500 ml/2 cups plus 2 tablespoons of the juice and refrigerate any leftovers for drinking. Stir the lime juice, sugar and rosewater into the pomegranate juice until the sugar has dissolved.

Knock out the seeds from the reserved pomegranate half and divide them between the moulds, then pour in the juice. Add the sticks in an upright position at this stage, or freeze first for a while until the mixture is firm enough to hold the sticks straight. Freeze for 4–6 hours until frozen.

When you are ready to serve, dip the moulds into hot water for a second or two, then gently pull out the popsicles. Decorate with fresh and dried rose petals and lime wedges, if you like.

CREAMY

BUTTERMILK, RASPBERRY AND PISTACHIO POPS

These frozen treats are an enticing combination of tangy, fresh and sweet. They are sweetened with low-GI agave syrup which is now widely available - honey can also be substituted. Dipping these into chopped pistachios to serve gives a lovely nutty, crunchy finish.

250 ml/1 cup plus 1 tablespoon Greek yogurt

250 ml/1 cup plus 1 tablespoon buttermilk

150 ml/⅔ cup agave syrup

125 g/4½ oz. fresh raspberries

25 g/1 oz. finely chopped, unsalted pistachio nuts

6 popsicle moulds and sticks

MAKES 6

Put the yogurt, buttermilk and agave syrup in a bowl and whisk together until just combined.

Divide the raspberries evenly between the moulds and then fill them up with the buttermilk mixture.

Add the sticks in an upright position at this stage, or freeze first for a while until the mixture is firm enough to hold the sticks straight. Freeze for 4–6 hours until frozen.

When you are ready to serve, dip the moulds into hot water for a second or two, then gently pull out the popsicles.

Dip the ends of the popsicles in the chopped pistachio nuts to serve.

TIRAMISU POPSICLES

Here, almond, coffee and chocolate ice creams are dipped into melted chocolate and coated in crushed biscuits/cookies. Delicious!

1 tablespoon cocoa powder

1 tablespoon instant espresso powder

2 tablespoons boiling water

250 g/1 cup mascarpone

300 ml/1¼ cups double/ heavy cream

50 ml/3½ tablespoons milk

3 tablespoons icing/ confectioners' sugar

½ teaspoon almond extract

100 g/3½ oz. dark/ bittersweet chocolate, chopped

25 g/1 oz. Savoiardi biscuits/cookies, crushed

6 small popsicle moulds and sticks

baking sheet, lined with baking parchment

MAKES 6 SMALL

Dissolve the cocoa powder and the espresso powder separately in 1 tablespoon of boiling water each. Let them cool.

Combine the mascarpone, cream, milk, sugar and almond extract in a food processor and blend until smooth. Measure and divide evenly into three bowls. Stir the cocoa into one and the coffee into another, leaving one plain.

Divide the plain cream between the moulds. Freeze for 1 hour or until firm. Add the coffee layer and freeze for 30 minutes or until firm enough to hold the sticks upright. Gently add the sticks and freeze for another 30 minutes until firm. Finally, add the chocolate cream mixture and freeze for 4–6 hours until frozen.

20 minutes before you are ready to serve, put the prepared baking sheet into the freezer. Meanwhile, melt the chocolate in a heatproof bowl set over a pan of barely simmering water. Make sure the base of the bowl does not touch the water. After 10 minutes, dip the moulds quickly into hot water, then gently pull out the popsicles. Immediately dip the ends into the melted chocolate and then into the crushed biscuits/cookies. Place the popsicles on the prepared tray and return to the freezer for 10 minutes to set.

SALTED BANOFFEE ICE CREAMS

I'm not sure what there is to say about this heavenly combination other than make it, then freeze it and eat it - you will not regret it!

4 tablespoons golden/corn syrup

1 tablespoon cocoa powder

2 bananas, peeled and chopped

300 ml/1⅓ cups double/heavy cream

25 g/2 tablespoons caster/granulated sugar

25 g/1 oz. blanched almonds

1 tablespoon cold water

a little sea salt

4 tablespoons ready-made caramel sauce

8 popsicle moulds and sticks

2 small baking sheets, 1 lined with foil and 1 lined with baking parchment

MAKES 8

Place 3 tablespoons of the syrup and the cocoa powder into a bowl and stir well until smooth.

Place the bananas, cream and sugar into a blender and blend until completely smooth. Pour the banana cream into the moulds. Drizzle in the cocoa syrup and swirl through with a skewer to create a ripple effect.

Add the sticks in an upright position at this stage, or freeze first for a while until the mixture is firm enough to hold the sticks straight. Freeze for 4–6 hours until frozen.

Meanwhile, place the almonds, water and remaining 1 tablespoon syrup in a small frying pan/skillet. Heat gently until the syrup begins to boil. Boil for 3–4 minutes, without stirring, until the almonds are glazed. Transfer the nuts to the foiled baking sheet and sprinkle with the salt. Cool completely, then roughly chop.

20 minutes before you are ready to serve, put the paper-lined baking sheet into the freezer. After 10 minutes, dip the moulds quickly into hot water, then gently pull out the popsicles. Place the popsicles on the chilled sheet and drizzle over the caramel. Top with the glazed nuts. Freeze again for 10 minutes to set.

AVOCADO MILKSHAKE POPSICLES

These avocado ice pops are inspired by the popular Vietnamese avocado milkshake and make a refreshing and indulgent treat. They taste like a rich, dairy ice cream but are a little lighter thanks to the addition of fat-free sweetened condensed milk.

4 medium-sized ripe avocados
1 tablespoon finely grated orange zest
250 ml/1 cup plus 1 tablespoon light/fat-free condensed milk (sweetened)

10 small popsicle moulds or straight-sided plastic glasses and sticks

MAKES 10 SMALL

Use a spoon to remove the flesh from the avocados, discarding the skin and pit. Cut off any brown bits. Put the avocado flesh, orange zest and light/fat-free condensed milk in a blender and process until smooth.

Pour the mixture into the moulds or plastic glasses. Add the sticks in an upright position at this stage, or freeze first for a while until the mixture is firm enough to hold the sticks straight. Freeze for 4–6 hours until frozen.

When you are ready to serve, dip the moulds into hot water for a second or two, then gently pull out the popsicles.

EXTREME CHOCOLATE
AND HAZELNUT STICKS

A rich chocolate mousse coated in dark/bittersweet chocolate topped off with toasted chopped hazelnuts - these are dangerously good.

75 g/¾ stick unsalted butter

175 g/6 oz. milk/ semisweet chocolate (chips or chopped)

3 eggs, separated

30 g/2½ tablespoons caster/superfine sugar

200 g/7 oz. dark/ bittersweet chocolate, chopped, 75% cocoa solids

50 ml/3½ tablespoons cold water

25 g/1 oz. hazelnuts, toasted and finely chopped

6 popsicle moulds and sticks

small baking sheet, lined with baking parchment

MAKES 6

Melt the butter and milk/semisweet chocolate gently together in a small saucepan. Remove from the heat.

Whisk the egg whites with a hand-held electric whisk to stiff peaks, then whisk in the sugar until thick. Beat the egg yolks into the chocolate-butter mix and then fold in the egg whites until just combined. Divide the mixture between the moulds. Add the sticks in an upright position at this stage, or freeze first for a while until the mixture is firm enough to hold the sticks straight. Freeze for 4–6 hours.

20 minutes before you are ready to serve, put the prepared baking sheet into the freezer. Meanwhile, combine the chocolate and water in a saucepan over a very low heat, stirring, until melted and smooth. Let it cool slightly.

After 10 minutes, dip the moulds quickly into hot water, then gently pull out the popsicles. Immediately pour the melted chocolate sauce over the popsicles, coating as much of them as you can. Quickly place the popsicles on the prepared baking sheet and scatter over the hazelnuts. Freeze again for 10 minutes until set before serving.

STRAWBERRY AND TOASTED MARSHMALLOW POPS

These delectable treats taste like s'mores sandwiched between fresh strawberry ice cream. If you are lucky enough to have any of the toasted marshmallow cream left over, just eat it as it is!

300 g/10½ oz. strawberries, hulled and halved

50 g/¼ cup caster/ granulated sugar

200 g/scant 1 cup Greek yogurt

25 g/1 oz. large marshmallows

1 teaspoon pure vanilla extract

100 ml/⅓ cup plus 1 tablespoon double/ heavy cream, whipped until slightly thickened

8 popsicle moulds and sticks

metal skewers

MAKES 8

Dice 50 g/1¾ oz. of the strawberries, and reserve for later. Place the remaining strawberries in a bowl and stir in the sugar. Set aside for 1 hour. Place the sugared strawberries and their juices in a blender and blend until smooth. Add the yogurt and blend. Divide half the strawberry yogurt between the moulds, reserving and refrigerating the rest. Add the sticks in an upright position, or freeze first until the mixture is firm enough to hold the sticks straight. Freeze for 1 hour until frozen.

Meanwhile, thread the marshmallows onto the skewers and toast over a flame (or under a grill/broiler) until caramelized but not melted. Set aside to cool, then roughly chop.

Fold the marshmallows, vanilla and reserved strawberries into the lightly whipped cream. Divide between the moulds and return to the freezer for about 1 hour until firm. Pour in the remaining strawberry yogurt and freeze for 4–6 hours until completely frozen.

When ready to serve, dip the moulds quickly into hot water, then pull out the popsicles.

BLUEBERRY AND LAVENDER CHEESECAKE POPSICLES

Another popular dessert layered in a mould and frozen into popsicle form. Blueberries pair perfectly with lavender and this aromatic floral adds an exotic flourish to an already wickedly good ice pop.

300 g/1⅓ cups cream cheese

200 ml/generous ¾ cup double/heavy cream

freshly squeezed juice of ½ lemon

60 g/⅓ cup minus 1 teaspoon caster/granulated sugar

150 g/5½ oz. fresh blueberries

1 teaspoon edible dried lavender flowers

50 g/1¾ oz. speculoos or ginger biscuits/cookies

15 g/1 tablespoon butter, melted

8 popsicle moulds and sticks

MAKES 8

Place the cream cheese, cream, lemon juice and half the sugar in a food processor and blend until smooth. Refrigerate.

Place the remaining sugar, the blueberries and lavender flowers in a small saucepan over a low-medium heat, stirring until the sugar has dissolved. Simmer gently for a further 5 minutes, then let it cool completely.

Divide the cooled blueberry mixture between the moulds. Add the sticks in an upright position, or freeze first for a while until the mixture is firm enough to hold the sticks straight. Freeze for 1 hour or until frozen.

Pour the layer of cream cheese mixture into the moulds and freeze again for 1 hour or until firm.

Meanwhile, put the biscuits/cookies and melted butter in a food processor and blend to fine crumbs. Divide between the moulds and press down. Freeze again for 4–6 hours.

When you are ready to serve, dip the moulds into hot water for a second or two, then gently pull out the popsicles.

SOFT ICES

KEFIR AND DATE CONES

Kefir is a cultured, fermented milk drink with a slightly sour, tart taste. It has the texture of thin yogurt and is full of healthy probiotics, which are excellent for maintaining a healthy gut. Kefir is now pretty widely available from health food stores and larger supermarkets, but plain yogurt can be substituted here, if you prefer.

750 ml/3¼ cups kefir (pure kefir rather than the kefir drink)

150 g/5½ oz. pitted and chopped Medjool dates

1–2 teaspoons almond extract, to taste

ice cream cones, to serve

finely grated dark/ bittersweet chocolate, to serve

ice-cream machine (optional)

piping/pastry bag with a fluted or plain nozzle/tip (optional)

MAKES APPROX. 900 ML/SCANT 4 CUPS

Place all the ingredients, except the cones and chocolate, in a blender and blend until completely smooth.

If you have an ice-cream machine, use this to churn the mixture according to the manufacturer's instructions. Or, if you are not using a machine, transfer the mixture to a freezerproof container. Freeze for 2 hours, then stir well with a fork to break up the ice crystals. Return to the freezer and continue to stir well every hour until the ice cream is smooth and frozen. It should take about 6 hours in total.

If you want to serve with a very neat finish, then transfer your ice cream to the piping/ pastry bag. (If you have used an ice-cream machine, then place the filled bag in the freezer for 10 minutes to firm up a bit more.) Pipe the mixture directly into your cones. Alternatively, you can just use an ice-cream scoop or spoon.

Serve sprinkled with a little finely grated dark/ bittersweet chocolate.

BUTTERMILK WHIRLS
WITH RASPBERRY SAUCE

I love the tang and lightness that buttermilk adds to ice cream, both in flavour and texture, making it perfect for piping. It is delicious drizzled with this freshly-made raspberry sauce.

500 ml/2 cups plus
    2 tablespoons
    buttermilk
250 ml/1 cup plus 1
    tablespoon double/
    heavy cream
60 ml/¼ cup maple
    syrup
2 teaspoons pure vanilla
    extract

RASPBERRY SAUCE
100 g/3½ oz. frozen
    raspberries
1 tablespoon maple
    syrup

*ice-cream machine
    (optional)*

*piping/pastry bag
    with a fluted or plain
    nozzle/tip (optional)*

MAKES APPROX.
750 ML/3¼ CUPS

For the sauce, place the raspberries in a small saucepan with the maple syrup over a low heat until softened. Turn up the heat and bring to the boil, stirring, until the fruit has broken down. Remove from the heat, then pass the sauce through a sieve/strainer. Leave to cool.

Whisk the buttermilk, cream, syrup and vanilla together until smooth. If you have an ice-cream machine, use this to churn the mixture according to the manufacturer's instructions. If you are not using a machine, transfer the mixture to a freezerproof container. Freeze for 2 hours, then stir well with a fork to break up the ice crystals. Return to the freezer and stir every hour until the ice cream is smooth and frozen. It should take about 6 hours in total.

If you want to serve with a neat finish, then transfer your ice cream to the piping/pastry bag. (If you have used an ice-cream machine, then place the filled bag in the freezer for 10 minutes to firm up a bit more.) Pipe the ice cream into cups or serving dishes. Alternatively, you can just use an ice-cream scoop or spoon. Serve drizzled with the raspberry sauce.

AVOCADO AND PISTACHIO SOFTIES

One of my favourite flavours of ice cream - but a whole lot healthier and vegan! I like to add pistachio paste for the extra colour, but if you can't find any, then just use almond extract, the flavour is very similar.

1 large avocado (about
200 g/7 oz.)
500 ml/2 cups plus
2 tablespoons almond
milk
60 g/2¼ oz. unsalted
shelled pistachio nuts,
chopped, plus extra
to serve
125 ml/½ cup coconut
milk
150 g/⅔ cup agave syrup
or clear honey
2 teaspoons pistachio
paste or a few drops
of almond extract
1 tablespoon freshly
squeezed lemon juice
ice cream cones, to serve
(optional)

*ice-cream machine
(optional)*

**MAKES APPROX.
750 ML/3¹/4 CUPS**

Remove the pit from the avocado and scoop the flesh into a blender. Add the almond milk, pistachio nuts, coconut milk, agave syrup (or honey) and either the pistachio paste or almond extract. Blend until really smooth. Add the lemon juice and blend briefly to combine.

If you have an ice-cream machine, use this to churn the mixture according to the manufacturer's instructions. Or, if you are not using a machine, transfer the mixture to a freezerproof container. Freeze for 2 hours, then stir very thoroughly with a fork to break up the ice crystals. Return to the freezer and continue to stir well every hour until the ice cream is smooth and frozen. It should take about 6 hours in total.

Spoon the ice cream into serving dishes or cones and sprinkle with extra chopped pistachios to serve.

CASHEW BUTTER ICE CREAM

Cashew butter is swirled through this ice cream to give a lovely ripple effect. Drizzle with extra cashew butter to serve, if you like.

180 g/1 cup xylitol

6 egg yolks

400 ml/1¾ cups rice milk

400 ml/1¾ cups soy cream

seeds from 1 vanilla pod/bean

200 g/1 scant cup cashew butter (available in supermarkets and health food stores)

3 tablespoons agave syrup

ice-cream machine (optional)

MAKES APPROX. 1 LITRE/QUART

Put the xylitol and egg yolks in a bowl and, using an electric whisk, whisk until light, fluffy and pale yellow. Set aside for a moment.

Combine the milk, soy cream and vanilla in a heavy-based saucepan. Bring to the boil for 1 minute. Remove from heat and cool slightly.

Pour the warm cream mixture into the egg mixture, whisking constantly and vigorously to combine. Pour the mixture back into the saucepan over a low heat. Using a plastic spatula, stir the mixture constantly in a figure-of-eight motion for 5–10 minutes until thickened. It should be thick enough to coat the back of a spoon.

If you have an ice-cream machine, use this to churn the mixture according to the manufacturer's instructions. If you don't have an ice-cream machine, pour the mixture into a freezerproof container and freeze. After 30 minutes, remove from the freezer and stir well to break up the ice crystals. Repeat this process at 30-minute intervals until you have a smooth ice cream. It should take about 6 hours.

Mix together the cashew butter and agave syrup and stir through the ice cream to create swirls, then freeze for 30 minutes to fully set.

COCONUT FROZEN YOGURT WITH STRAWBERRIES

Frozen yogurt is going through a bit of a renaissance at the moment and it's not hard to see why. Fresh and light with only a fraction of the fat of ice cream, it is the natural choice for the health-conscious. It is still made with dairy though, so I came up with this recipe using soy yogurt and coconut milk, which is truly delicious.

700 ml/3¼ cups plain soy yogurt

340 ml/scant 1½ cups coconut milk

100 ml/⅓ cup plus 1 tablespoon agave syrup

2 teaspoons freshly squeezed lemon juice

TO SERVE

fresh strawberries

desiccated/dried shredded coconut

ice-cream machine (optional)

MAKES SCANT 1 LITRE/QUART

Combine the soy yogurt, coconut milk, agave syrup and lemon juice in a bowl and mix until nice and smooth.

If you have an ice-cream machine, use this to churn the mixture according to the manufacturer's instructions. Or, if you are not using a machine, pour the mixture into a freezerproof container and freeze. After 30 minutes, remove from the freezer and whisk thoroughly to break up the ice crystals. Return to the freezer and repeat this process every 30 minutes until completely frozen, but not rock hard, as you want to be able to scoop it out easily. It should take about 6 hours.

Scoop the frozen yogurt into serving bowls or a serving dish and top with strawberries and desiccated/dried shredded coconut.

SUGAR-FREE MOJITO SORBET

This is the perfect, refreshing light treat with the clean, simple flavours of mint and lime. Try serving it to guests after a rich or spicy meal as a palate cleanser.

180 g/1 cup xylitol
5 sprigs of fresh mint
    plus 2 tablespoons
    freshly chopped leaves
finely grated zest and
    freshly squeezed juice
    of 2 limes

ice-cream machine
    (optional)

**MAKES APPROX.
500 ML/2 CUPS**

Combine 500 ml/2 cups plus 2 tablespoons water, the xylitol and mint sprigs in a saucepan and bring to the boil. Reduce the heat to low and simmer for 5 minutes.

Remove from the heat and strain the liquid into a bowl, squeezing as much liquid as possible out of the mint. Immediately, while the liquid is still hot, add the lime zest. Allow the mixture to cool slightly, then stir in the lime juice and chopped mint leaves. Refrigerate to cool thoroughly.

If you have an ice-cream machine, use this to churn the mixture according to the manufacturer's instructions. If you are not using an ice-cream machine, pour the mixture into a freezerproof container and freeze. After 20 minutes, remove the container from the freezer and stir thoroughly with a fork to break up the ice crystals. Return to the freezer and repeat this process every 20 minutes for about 2 hours until smooth. Note: the final texture of this sorbet is quite soft.

INDEX